# Lise Meitner

## Pioneer of Nuclear Fission

*Titles in the Great Minds of Science series:*

**ALBERT EINSTEIN**
**Physicist and Genius**
Paperback ISBN 0-7660-1864-4
Library Ed. ISBN 0-89490-480-9

**ALEXANDER FLEMING**
**The Man Who Discovered Penicillin**
Library Ed. ISBN 0-7660-1998-5

**ANTOINE LAVOISIER**
**Founder of Modern Chemistry**
Paperback ISBN 0-7660-1865-2
Library Ed. ISBN 0-89490-785-9

**ANTONI van LEEUWENHOEK**
**First to See Microscopic Life**
Paperback ISBN 0-7660-1866-0
Library Ed. ISBN 0-89490-680-1

**CARL LINNAEUS**
**Father of Classification**
Paperback ISBN 0-7660-1867-9
Library Ed. ISBN 0-89490-786-7

**CHARLES DARWIN**
**Naturalist**
Paperback ISBN 0-7660-1868-7
Library Ed. ISBN 0-89490-476-0

**COPERNICUS**
**Founder of Modern Astronomy**
Library Ed. ISBN 0-7660-1755-9

**EDWIN HUBBLE**
**Discoverer of Galaxies**
Paperback ISBN 0-7660-1869-5
Library Ed. ISBN 0-89490-934-7

**GALILEO**
**Astronomer and Physicist**
Paperback ISBN 0-7660-1870-9
Library Ed. ISBN 0-89490-787-5

**GREGOR MENDEL**
**Father of Genetics**
Paperback ISBN 0-7660-1871-7
Library Ed. ISBN 0-89490-789-1

**ISSAC NEWTON**
**The Greatest Scientist of All Time**
Paperback ISBN 0-7660-1872-5
Library Ed. ISBN 0-89490-681-X

**THE LEAKEYS**
**Uncovering the Origins of Humankind**
Paperback ISBN 0-7660-1873-3
Library Ed. ISBN 0-89490-788-3

**LISE MEITNER**
**Pioneer of Nuclear Fission**
Library Ed. ISBN 0-7660-1756-7

**LOUIS PASTEUR**
**Disease Fighter**
Paperback ISBN 0-7660-1874-1
Library Ed. ISBN 0-89490-790-5

**MARIE CURIE**
**Discoverer of Radium**
Paperback ISBN 0-7660-1875-X
Library Ed. ISBN 0-89490-477-9

**NIELS BOHR**
**Scientist and Humanitarian**
Library Ed. ISBN 0-7660-1997-7

**TYCHO BRAHE**
**Astronomer**
Library Ed. ISBN 0-7660-1757-5

**WILLIAM HARVEY**
**Discoverer of How Blood Circulates**
Paperback ISBN 0-7660-1876-8
Library Ed. ISBN 0-89490-481-7

GREAT MINDS OF SCIENCE

# Lise Meitner

## Pioneer of Nuclear Fission

Janet Hamilton

**Enslow Publishers, Inc.**

40 Industrial Road                    PO Box 38
Box 398                               Aldershot
Berkeley Heights, NJ  07922    Hants GU12 6BP
USA                                        UK

http://www.enslow.com

*For my husband, William, and my daughters,*
*Christine and Katherine.*

**Library of Congress Cataloging-in-Publication Data**

Hamilton, Janet.
    Lise Meitner : pioneer of nuclear fission / Janet Hamilton.
        p. cm. — (Great minds of science)
    Includes bibliographical references and index.
    ISBN 0-7660-1756-7
    1. Meitner, Lise, 1878–1968—Juvenile literature. 2. Physicists—
Germany—Biography—Juvenile literature. 3. Women physicists—
Germany—Biography—Juvenile literature. 4. Nuclear fission—
Juvenile literature. [1. Meitner, Lise, 1878–1968. 2. Physicists.
3. Women—Biography.] I. Title. II. Series.
    QC774 .M4 H35 2002
    539'.092—dc21

                                                        2001002119

Printed in the United States of America

10 9 8 7 6 5 4 3 2 1

**To Our Readers:** We have done our best to make sure all Internet addresses
in this book were active and appropriate when we went to press. However,
the author and the publisher have no control over and assume no liability
for the material available on those Internet sites or on other Web sites they
may link to. Any comments or suggestions can be sent by e-mail to
comments@enslow.com or to the address on the back cover.

**Illustration Credits:** Albert Einstein Archives, The Hebrew University
of Jerusalem Israel, p. 63; Churchill Archives Centre, Meitner Papers,
MTNR 8, pp. 8, 12, 17, 19, 31, 34, 36, 41, 44, 50, 52, 54, 73, 80, 91,
100, 102, 105; David Torsiello, p. 110; Enslow Publishers, Inc., pp. 15,
23, 25, 83, 93; German Information Center, p. 27; National Archives,
pp. 60, 97.

**Cover Illustration:** © Corel Corporation (background); Churchill
Archives Centre, Meitner Papers, MTNR 8 (inset).

# Contents

**1** A Chain of Events . . . . . . . . . . .   7

**2** Early Years . . . . . . . . . . . . . .   11

**3** Studying Radiation . . . . . . . . .   21

**4** Moving to Berlin . . . . . . . . . . .   29

**5** The Great War . . . . . . . . . . . .   38

**6** The Calm Before the Storm . . . .   47

**7** The Rise of the Nazis . . . . . . . .   57

**8** Escape from Germany . . . . . . . .   67

**9** Splitting the Atom . . . . . . . . . .   76

**10** World War II . . . . . . . . . . . . . .   87

**11** Meitner's Legacy . . . . . . . . . .   95

Activities . . . . . . . . . . . . . . . .   107

Chronology . . . . . . . . . . . . . .   113

Chapter Notes . . . . . . . . . . . .   115

Glossary . . . . . . . . . . . . . . . .   120

Further Reading . . . . . . . . . . .   124

Internet Addresses . . . . . . . . .   125

Index . . . . . . . . . . . . . . . . . .   126

# 1

# A Chain of Events

ON AUGUST 6, 1945, THE WORLD WAS shocked when the United States dropped an atomic bomb on the city of Hiroshima in Japan. The U.S. had been at war with Japan since December 1941. Much of the rest of the world had been at war since 1939. World War II had ended in Europe in May, but the fighting in the Pacific had continued.

During the war there had been rumors that an atomic bomb was being developed in the United States or Germany. This bomb would use nuclear fission for energy. Nuclear fission is a process in which atoms are split. An atom can be

*Lise Meitner enjoys a cup of tea during a visit to Cambridge, England in 1928.*

split with a neutron, which is a part of an atom. When an atom is split, it gives off a great deal of energy. In addition, a few other neutrons are released. These neutrons go on to split other atoms. This is called a chain reaction.

At the beginning of the twentieth century, scientists knew very little about the atom. Between 1900 and the beginning of World War II in 1939, much had been discovered. But there was still not enough information to make the bomb. At the end of 1938, though, the crucial discovery of fission was made.

This was a remarkable discovery. Even more remarkable was that the woman who made it, Lise Meitner, was living in exile. Because of the war, she had been forced to leave Germany, where she had lived and worked for thirty years. With hardly more than the clothes on her back, she had escaped to Sweden. She left behind all her scientific equipment, her books, and her colleagues. In spite of all this, she managed to solve a problem that had puzzled scientists for many years.

Lise Meitner was not interested in making bombs. When she was asked by the U.S. government to work for the Manhattan Project, the top secret quest to build an atomic bomb, she turned them down.[1] Her reason for exploring the atom and fission was to learn more. All her life she had a passion for learning. Her passion led to the creation of weapons that changed the world. But it also led to a greater understanding of some of the smallest particles in the universe.

# Early Years

LISE MEITNER WAS BORN IN VIENNA, Austria, on November 7, 1878. Vienna was an exciting city. Lise's parents, Phillipp and Hedwig Meitner, were very much a part of it. Phillipp Meitner was one of the first Jewish men to be allowed to become a lawyer in Austria. Jews in Austria had not always had the same rights as Christians. The late 1800s was a time of great change however, and Austrian lawyers were busy making many reforms. The Meitner home was filled with interesting visitors who were helping to reshape the country. Lise was the third of eight children, so their comfortable apartment was always a lively place.

*Phillipp Meitner, the father of Lise Meitner, was one of the first Jewish men to practice law in Austria.*

Vienna was a city filled with musicians and artists. Although the Meitners did not have a lot of money to support their large family, all the children took music lessons. Lise's older sister, Auguste, became a concert pianist.

Lise's other brothers and sisters also grew up to have distinguished careers. Education was very important to the Meitner family. Another sister, Frida, earned a Ph.D. in physics and became a college professor. One of her brothers, Walther, earned a Ph.D. in chemistry. Another, Fritz, became an engineer.[1]

It was not easy for the girls to get a good education, though. When Lise was fourteen she was no longer allowed to go to school. At the time, Viennese schools did not allow girls to attend gymnasiums. Gymnasiums were the difficult schools that prepared boys for a university education. Although Lise loved math and science, she was expected to stay home until she got married, or she could teach a subject that did not require a university education. Lise decided to study French. She also passed her time tutoring to earn money for her older sister's advanced music lessons.

Fortunately, in 1897, laws were changed to allow girls to pursue higher education. One evening Lise approached her father and quietly asked for his permission to prepare to enter the university. He agreed, as long as she first acquired a license to teach so that she would have a way to support herself.

Lise began an intensive study with other girls who wanted to go to a university. In addition to getting her license to teach French, she worked hard to learn math and science. Her group spent two years studying subjects that boys attending a gymnasium would have taken eight years to learn. Lise's brothers and sisters teased her about studying so hard. They would make jokes if she walked across the living room without a book in her hand.[2] At the end of the two years, Lise took the *Matura* (the entrance examination for the university) with thirteen other girls. She was one of only four who passed.

Lise Meitner entered the University of

# Europe Before World War I, 1914

*A map showing the boundaries of Europe prior to World War I.*

Vienna in October 1901, just before her twenty-third birthday. She felt that she had lost so much time that she needed to work extra hard to catch up. She enrolled in twenty-five hours of classes a week, studying calculus, physics, chemistry, and botany. Her work was so difficult and time-consuming that she often had to struggle to stay awake in class.

Although Meitner enjoyed all her studies, by the second half of her first year at the university she had decided to concentrate on physics. At that time there were not many physicists in the world, and most of them worked in teaching or research. As a woman, Meitner's chances of finding work in the field of physics were even slimmer. But she knew she loved the subject enough to try to make it her life's work.

During her second year at the university, Meitner began studying physics in earnest. This meant studying different topics on how nature works, including electricity, magnetism, heat, light, sound, and matter. She enjoyed her work. Many of her courses were taught by Ludwig

*Hedwig Skovran Meitner, mother of Lise Meitner.*

Boltzmann. Boltzmann was a large, intense man and a brilliant physicist. He could laugh at the mistakes he made during his lectures, but he offered his students "everything I have: myself, my entire way of thinking and feeling." He asked in return for their "strict attention, iron discipline, tireless strength of mind."[3] From him, Lise came to see physics as a search for ultimate truth.[4]

By the summer of 1905 Lise had completed all her course work at the university. She was ready to move on to the research project she would need to complete to get her doctoral degree. Her research was to find out if heat is conducted through a solid in a similar way to electricity. She wrote a paper, or thesis, on her findings. This paper was published by the Vienna Physics Institute. After an oral examination she graduated summa cum laude (with highest honors) with a doctoral degree in physics in February 1906.

Even though she had an advanced physics degree, it was difficult for Lise to find a place to work. A theoretical physicist who had graduated a few years earlier, Paul Ehrenfest, heard of her work. During her last year of school, he asked her to look at a paper written by physicist Lord Rayleigh, that described an experiment he could not explain. Lise explained it and predicted

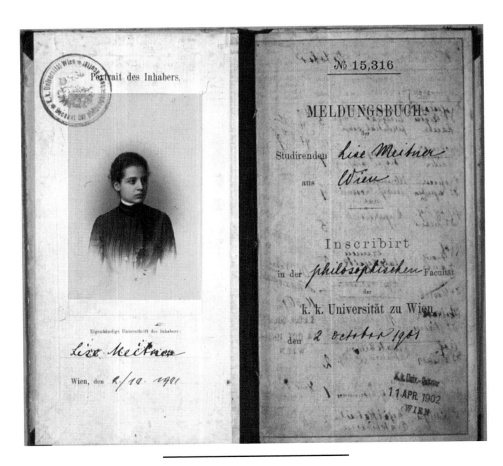

*Lise Meitner's University pass from the University of Vienna.*

some other results, which she was able to prove through a series of experiments. This work showed that she was able to conduct research and led to her first independent publication in a scientific journal. Meitner was beginning to gain recognition for her work. Still, forging a career in physics would be very difficult.

# Studying Radiation

AFTER HER WORK WITH EHRENFEST, LISE Meitner was again unsure what to do. Most Austrian physicists worked in the universities, beginning at the lowest level, in a position called *Assistent*. There had never been a female *Assistent* in Austria, and it seemed unlikely that Lise would be able to get a position as one. She wrote to the Nobel prize-winning scientist Marie Curie in Paris, France, but Curie had no position available in her lab.

Finally, with no other options, Lise began teaching in a girls' school to earn money. She knew she did not want to teach, though. In the evenings she would return to her physics research. She worked without pay at the Institute for Theoretical Physics, the lab at the university that Professor Boltzmann had headed. He had recently died and been replaced by Stefan Meyer. The lab was run down, with an entrance that looked like a henhouse. Meitner often thought that if a fire broke out, few people would get out alive.[1] In spite of this, she spent as much time as she could in the lab. This is where she first became involved with research on radioactivity.

Natural radioactivity had been discovered by Antoine-Henri Becquerel in 1896. An element is radioactive when it emits particles or energy. Elements can become radioactive when their atoms transform or change. This process is also called radioactive decay. To understand it, it is important to know the structure of an atom.

Each atom has a core called a nucleus. The nucleus is made up of protons and neutrons. Protons have a positive charge. Neutrons have no charge and are neutral. Circling the nucleus

# Basic Model of the Atom

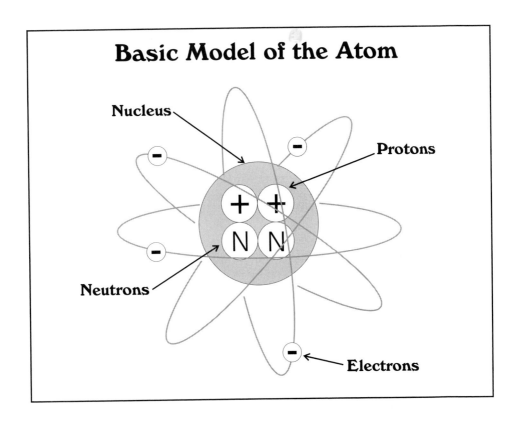

Nucleus

Protons

Neutrons

Electrons

are electrons. Electrons have a negative charge. Usually, an atom will have the same number of electrons as protons. Chemical elements are identified by their atomic number. This number tells us the number of protons in the nucleus of its atom. For instance, a hydrogen atom has one proton in its nucleus, so it has an atomic number of one.

The mass number of an element is the

number of protons plus the number of neutrons in the nucleus. Ordinary hydrogen has one proton and no neutrons, so its mass number is also one. Deuterium is a heavier form of hydrogen. It has one proton and one neutron. Its mass number is two. Tritium is a radioactive form of hydrogen. It has one proton and two neutrons, giving it an atomic mass of three. All three substances have the same atomic number but different mass numbers. They are called isotopes. Ordinary hydrogen, deuterium, and tritium are isotopes of hydrogen.

In 1900, shortly before Lise entered the university, there were five known radioactive elements. By 1916, there were more than twenty. Part of the reason for such a big jump was that scientists did not understand that isotopes were just different forms of the same element. They treated the radioactive isotopes they were discovering as new elements.

Three main types of radiation can come from an element. The first is alpha radiation. This occurs when a nucleus gives off alpha particles.

An alpha particle is made up of two protons and two neutrons. This gives it a positive charge. Because of this particle's large size, it does not easily slip between the molecules of other substances. Therefore it is easy to contain. This makes it a very weak kind of radiation. It can be stopped by a couple pieces of paper.

The second type of radiation is called beta

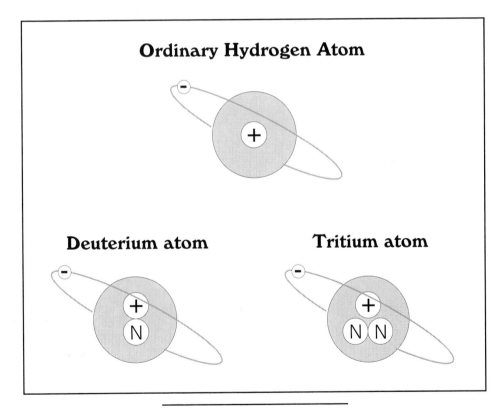

*Different types of hydrogen atoms.*

radiation. Beta particles are usually electrons. Sometimes, however, they can be positrons. Positrons are positively charged particles similar to electrons. Electrons and positrons are much smaller than protons and neutrons. Because of this, beta radiation is more penetrating. It can pass through heavier material than alpha particles can. This makes it a stronger kind of radiation. When alpha or beta radiation occurs, the atom changes and a new substance is formed.

The third type is gamma radiation. This is the most powerful form of radiation. Gamma rays have no charge.

At the university laboratory, Meitner studied the effects of alpha particles passing through matter. She wondered if the matter absorbed them or if they were scattered. She designed an experiment that showed they were scattered. The scattering increased with elements that had a larger atomic mass.

In 1906 the famous physicist Max Planck visited the lab where Meitner was working.

*Physicist Max Planck visited the laboratory where Lise Meitner was working in 1906. His visit inspired Meitner to move to Berlin so she could attend his lectures.*

Planck was from Berlin, Germany, and had done groundbreaking work with radiation. After meeting him, Meitner wanted to move to Berlin so that she could attend his lectures.

In June 1907 the results of Meitner's scattering experiments were published in the scientific journal *Physical Chemistry Journal*. With this success, she had the courage to approach her parents and ask them to support her going to Berlin to do research there. After they agreed to give her an allowance, she left for Berlin in September 1907.

# Moving to Berlin

WHEN LISE MEITNER ARRIVED AT THE University of Berlin, it was quickly becoming a center for young physicists. Part of the reason was Max Planck, the head of the theoretical physics department there. Indeed, he was the one who had inspired Meitner to go to Berlin. Planck had become famous in the early 1900s for his experiments with thermodynamics. Thermodynamics includes the study of how heat is absorbed and given off by different materials. He went on to win the Nobel prize for physics in 1918.

Planck was different from Meitner's first

mentor, Ludwig Boltzmann. The son of a Protestant minister, Planck was very modest and quiet. Until she got to know him, Meitner found his lectures somewhat dry. Eventually she realized he was reserved and led a simple life, and his lectures reflected this. She learned a great deal about physics from him.

Meitner wanted to continue her research on radioactivity. She approached Heinrich Rubens, the head of the university's department of experimental physics, to see about using a laboratory to do her research. He told her that the only space he had was in his lab, working under him. Meitner wanted to do independent research. While she was considering how she could turn down his offer without offending him, a young chemist named Otto Hahn came into the office. Hahn was interested in Meitner's work. Meitner believed they could collaborate. Hahn was her age and had a very informal manner. This made her feel comfortable about asking him questions.[1]

Otto Hahn had done a good deal of research

on radioactivity in Canada, working under the famous British physicist Ernest Rutherford. He had been hired to work at the Berlin Institute, which was not far from the University of Berlin. The head of this institute was Emil Fischer. Fischer did not like having women working in his labs. He claimed that he had once worked

*Otto Hahn and Lise Meitner at work in the lab in 1908. Upon meeting the young chemist Hahn, Meitner realized the two of them could work well together.*

with a Russian woman who had an elaborate hairdo, and he was always worried her hair would catch fire.[2] Apparently he did not have the same concern for his own beard.

Finally, with Otto Hahn's encouragement, Fischer allowed Meitner to set up a lab in an old carpenter's wood shop in the basement of the Berlin Institute. Meitner agreed that she would not go into the rest of the building, including Hahn's lab. She had to go down the street to a hotel to use the bathroom. Meitner and Hahn would meet in the evenings to do their work together, after Hahn had spent the day working at the institute and Meitner had attended lectures at the university.

Meitner and Hahn soon had a lab set up with simple equipment where they could work together. They focused their research on beta radiation, studying the radiation from every known element. They were able to publish three articles together in 1908 and six more the following year. At the end of 1908, Ernest Rutherford won the Nobel prize for chemistry for his work in radioactivity. This made scientists take the subject more seriously.

Although Hahn and Meitner had a very friendly working relationship, their friendship did not extend much beyond their lab. Meitner found it easier to make friends at the university. She soon was comfortable with many of the physicists who worked with Max Planck. Often Planck would invite the group to his house, where he enjoyed running races and playing tag in his garden.[3]

Meitner became good friends with Planck's twin daughters, Grete and Emma, who were close to her age. Other women friends she met in Berlin were Eva von Bahr-Bergius, a Swedish physicist who worked with Heinrich Rubens and Elisabeth Schiemann, a botanist at the university's institute for plant research. Meitner enjoyed the outdoors and went on many picnics and long hikes with her friends. In the summer of 1913 she and Elisabeth took trains and hiked with knapsacks all the way from Munich, Germany, to Vienna. There they attended the annual meeting of the Society of German Scientists and Physicians.

Another way Meitner met other scientists was through Heinrich Rubens's weekly colloquiums for physicists. The scientists from the university would gather each Wednesday to hear a lecture. This allowed them to learn about work that was being done in all areas of physics. Meitner and Hahn presented some of their findings there.

*Lise Meitner stands as the lone woman in the center of this gathering of physicists.*

These gatherings went on for many years. The front seats were taken by the leading physicists, such as Max Planck and Albert Einstein. Meitner, Hahn, and many of their other colleagues would sit a few rows back.

Although Meitner was enjoying her friends and her work in Berlin, life was somewhat difficult for her. She had to live on a very small allowance from her family, and she still was not paid for her research work. She made a little extra by translating scientific articles from English into German, and she often wrote articles for popular science journals. Once she was asked to write an article for a German encyclopedia. When the editor found out she was a woman, he quickly took back his offer, saying he "would not think of printing an article written by a woman!"[4]

Gradually the situation for women in Germany began to improve. In 1909, women were finally allowed to attend the University of Berlin as full-fledged students. Immediately after that, Emil Fischer gave Meitner permission

*Lise Meitner (center) enjoys some time away from the lab, outdoors, with friends.*

to go into all parts of his chemistry institute during working hours. His respect for her work grew over the years, and he eventually recommended her for several professional positions.

In 1912, after five years of working together, Meitner and Hahn prepared to move to a new lab that had just been built. It was called the Kaiser Wilhelm Institute for Chemistry. The German government had decided to set up private academic research labs to encourage scientists. The labs were funded by private companies. Otto Hahn was offered a position as the head of a small radioactivity section with a salary of 5,000 marks a year. Meitner was invited to work in the lab as an unpaid guest.

Shortly before the move, Meitner was hired for her first paid position after five years in Berlin. (Imagine working five years with no salary!) Max Planck appointed her his *Assistent* late in 1912. Each week she corrected his class assignments for over two hundred students, and chose one student's paper to be read aloud in class.[5] This seemed to open the doors to other employment for her. Within a year, she had been given a salaried position at the new institute, leading the radioactivity section with Hahn.

# The Great War

FOR TWO YEARS LISE MEITNER'S LIFE WAS peaceful and productive. This period came to an abrupt end in the summer of 1914. In early August, World War I began. Although most Germans believed they would win the war in a few months, it dragged on for more than four years. The impact on Meitner was immediate. Otto Hahn, who had recently married Edith Junghaus, was drafted early on and ordered to go to Wittenberg, Germany. Many of Meitner's other colleagues at the Kaiser Wilhelm Institute (KWI) were also called up to fight.

Women were urged to do their part to help

win the war, and Meitner looked for opportunities to serve. At the end of the summer, she went back to Vienna to visit her family and say goodbye to her brothers who had enlisted. She wrote often to Hahn, trying to send cheerful letters about news around the KWI. In the fall she started studying human anatomy and X-ray technology at a local hospital. She also began research in her lab on the medical applications of X-rays.

Shortly before the war began, Meitner had been offered an academic position at the University of Prague in what is now the Czech Republic. It was an appealing offer with a good salary. Emil Fischer, director of the KWI, offered her a salary of 1,000 marks a year to try to keep her in Berlin. Meitner wanted to stay where she had friends and the work she loved, so she decided to stay in Berlin at the KWI.

By the following year, 1915, it became obvious that the war would not end quickly. There were few students or scientists at the KWI. Most of the men had enlisted, and the women were also doing war work. Meitner decided to enlist as an X-ray nurse-technician for the Austrian army. She spent several weeks in training, and then she was sent to a military hospital near the Russian front.

At the hospital she sometimes worked twenty-hour days. The work with X-rays did not take much time, so she was put to work assisting with operations on the wounded soldiers. This experience gave her a lifelong horror of war. Her letters home expressed these feelings:

> *"I never expected it to be as awful as it actually is. These poor people, who at best will be cripples, have the most horrible pains. One can hear their screams and groans as well as see their horrible wounds. . . . Since we are only about 40 km [25 miles] from the front we get only the most severely wounded here. I tell myself this for consolation. But one has one's own thoughts about war when one sees all this."*[1]

By early 1916, the fighting where Meitner was had slowed down. She requested a transfer and spent a short time in Austria and then in Poland. In each place she found her work using

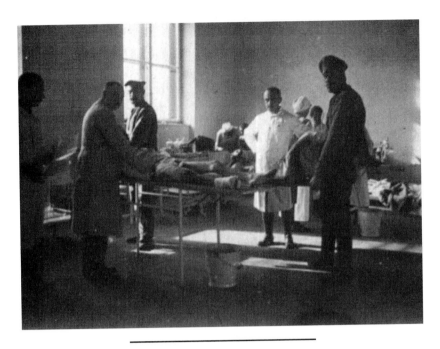

*Shortly after World War I began, Lise Meitner enlisted as an X-ray nurse technician for the Austrian army. She worked in a military hospital facility like the one pictured above.*

X-rays really was not needed. Finally, in September 1917, she left and returned to Berlin to work at the KWI.

Another reason for this return was that Meitner had heard disturbing news about the KWI. The Institute was being taken over for military research, and Hahn had written her that their section would be part of this research if she did not return. Hahn and Meitner were monitoring some materials in their lab for a long-term experiment. They were afraid these materials might be destroyed if Meitner was not there to protect them.

Before the war had started, Meitner and Hahn had spent quite a bit of time working on a special problem. They had begun by looking at a radioactive element called actinium. Actinium was extremely scarce and decayed fairly quickly. It was always found only with uranium-bearing minerals, so there seemed to be a link between uranium and actinium. Yet uranium did not produce actinium. They guessed that there might be an unknown element linking uranium and actinium. Meitner and Hahn had set out to discover that element.

The experiment they used to find this element would take several years. Some scientists believed that the missing element resembled a known element called tantalum. Meitner and Hahn separated the tantalum group from some uranium salts. They divided this into several samples and began watching them for signs of actinium.

Measuring radiation had been difficult in their old lab because it had been contaminated by other materials. Sometimes when radioactive materials come in contact with something, that item can continue to give off radiation for a long, long time. Soon radiation can be coming from many different things.

Meitner was known for being very strict about keeping her new lab clean. She hung rolls of toilet paper next to telephones and door handles to keep them clean. No one was allowed to shake hands. People who handled radioactive materials were allowed to sit only in special yellow chairs. Thanks to all her precautions, Meitner's lab was a place where even weak radioactive materials could be studied.

When Meitner returned to Berlin, she was eager to continue the project. She could tell from their radiation that some of her samples contained actinium. These were boiled in acid, filtered, and dried. Some of the solid that remained was mixed with an even stronger acid and boiled again. The small bit of solid left was assumed to contain the missing element.

All of this took months. Meitner and Hahn corresponded about the experiments regularly. During one of his leaves they were able to take final measurements on the solid and agreed that they had found the element they had been

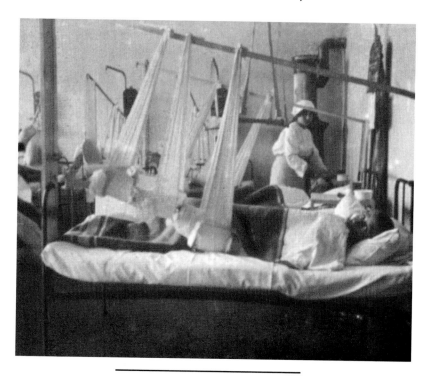

*Lise Meitner witnessed a great deal of the suffering of wounded soldiers during World War I. This experience may have been what influenced her decision to decline working on atomic bomb research years later.*

looking for. On March 16, 1918, they published a paper called "The Mother Substance of Actinium, a New Radioactive Element of Long Half-life" in the *Physical Chemistry Journal*.[2] They named the new element protactinium.

Eight months later, on November 11, 1918, the war ended with Germany's surrender. The kaiser left the throne, and the next several months were a chaotic time for Germany. Otto Hahn had spent the last years of the war using his knowledge of chemistry to develop poisonous gases for the Germans to use on their enemies. He was not able to return for months.

Although Germany was unstable after the war, the KWI continued to flourish. Science had been used throughout the war for military research. Now Germans wanted to use it to improve their industries and help get the country back on its feet. I.G. Farben, a German chemical company that had supported the institute during the last years of the war, continued to give money to keep it going. Meitner was put in charge of her own physics department at the end of 1918, near her fortieth birthday.

Although many Germans were interested in using science for industries, Meitner continued to pursue it for its own sake. There were other scientists who felt as she did. Albert Einstein, now working in Berlin, had refused to fight in the war and opposed war in general. Max Planck, who became a spokesperson for German science after the war said, "[I]n physics we labor not for the day, not for momentary success, but as it were, for eternity."[3] Even after enduring a horrible war, Meitner was still idealistic about physics. She still believed her work would positively influence people for many generations.

# The Calm Before the Storm

DESPITE THE DIFFICULT TIMES FACED BY Germany after World War I, Meitner's career was flourishing. In the summer of 1921 she took a trip to Copenhagen, Denmark, where she became good friends with the famous physicist Niels Bohr and his family. She also traveled to Sweden, where she spent a month working with another physicist, Manne Siegbahn. She also became friends with a visiting Dutch physicist, Dirk Coster. Both Siegbahn and Coster would later play an important role in Meitner's life.

It was a pleasure to visit Scandinavia after living in Berlin. The German economy was terrible. In the early 1920s, prices and salaries became incredibly inflated. Meitner and her colleagues received millions of marks in each paycheck. They would then rush out to spend it, since prices sometimes went up every few hours. They started receiving their paychecks every week, and then almost every day. Finally, in 1924, prices stabilized.[1]

Berlin was still an important center of science. Germans were very proud of their science and its contributions to the world. Unfortunately this pride had a dark side. A racist, nationalistic group called the Nazis started forming in the 1920s. The Nazis targeted several groups, especially Jews. Some members of these groups protested at Albert Einstein's public lectures in the early 1920s because Einstein was Jewish. They said his theory of relativity was false and that its importance had been exaggerated by what they called the "Jewish press."[2]

Although Lise Meitner had converted to Christianity in her twenties, she was from a

Jewish family. Fortunately, these extremist groups did not affect her much during these years. In 1921 Max Planck invited her to teach at the University of Berlin. She began lecturing the following year, and four years later became an assistant professor. She was required to have an oral examination, called a *Habilitation*, to qualify as a professor. This was given to her by Heinrich Rubens and her friend Max von Laue, who presented her with a certificate qualifying her to teach and give lectures. She did both for the next ten years.[3]

In addition to her new position, Meitner received a number of awards recognizing her work. In 1924 Max von Laue nominated her for the Leibniz Prize. The nomination was endorsed by Max Planck and Albert Einstein. She won the second place silver medal and was the first woman to win this coveted award. She also won the 1925 Ignaz Lieber Prize, awarded by the Academy of Sciences in Vienna.

The team of Otto Hahn and Lise Meitner was nominated for the Nobel prize several times.

Max Planck nominated Hahn for the chemistry prize in 1923, and he nominated Meitner and Hahn together every year from 1929 to 1934. They were also nominated by other scientists in 1924 and 1925.[4]

Even though Meitner and Hahn were recognized for the work they had done together, they were gradually working more and more independently of each other. Meitner's interests

*Lise Meitner sits in the front row of this picture, taken in 1920. Otto Hahn and Niels Bohr are among those also pictured.*

were more in teaching and research, while Hahn was involved with the administration of the KWI. He was in charge of giving out the funds that the institute received from the Association for German Science. Because the economy in Germany was so bad, this was a very difficult job. Hahn's good nature and ability to get along with people served him well in doing it.

Meitner was more interested in learning about the nucleus of the atom. In addition to her teaching at the University of Berlin and her research at the KWI, she often traveled to Niels Bohr's Copenhagen Institute in Denmark. There was a great exchange of ideas among physicists in different countries at this time.

These physicists had learned much about the structure of the atom during the previous twenty years. In 1911 Ernest Rutherford said that the atom had a small nucleus made of positively charged protons with negatively charged electrons orbiting around it. Two years later Niels Bohr diagramed how the electrons are arranged in shells, or levels, around the nucleus.

*The Kaiser Wilhelm Institute in Dahlem, 1930.*

Electrons with less energy are closer to the nucleus in lower levels. Those with more are in shells farther away in higher levels.

One way scientists study electrons is by looking at the light they give off in heated gases. All light is generated by electrons jumping from a higher level to a lower level. When this happens, photons of light are given off. Jumps made between different levels generate different colors (or wavelengths) of light.

We have all seen light separated into its different colors by raindrops or a prism. Scientists use a spectrometer to break light into its particular wavelengths or colors, called spectrum lines. They can then use these wavelengths to study electron motions in the atom. Meitner began to study all the known elements, analyzing their radiation properties using a spectrometer. Her work helped clarify how atoms break down and release energy.

Physicists in the 1920s were still having trouble understanding the nucleus of the atom, because neutrons had not been discovered. There was a lot of interest, though, in learning about the energy of the atom. Writers such as H.G. Wells wrote stories about using the power that came from atoms to run submarines and light cities. Others, including Einstein, thought the idea of atomic energy was impossible.[5]

The early 1930s was a time of many discoveries in the world of physics. One of the most important was the discovery of the neutron, the neutral particle in the nucleus of the atom. This was discovered in Great Britain in February 1932 by James Chadwick. Rutherford had first guessed that a similar particle existed back in 1920, but Chadwick was the first to prove it. Meitner was very interested in these findings. Chadwick visited her in Berlin in June, and later she did some experiments investigating how the neutron could cause nuclear reactions.[6]

*Lise Meitner and Otto Hahn at work together in their lab. Meitner and Hahn received Nobel prize nominations together in 1924, 1925, and every year from 1929 to 1934.*

Meitner also worked with a Wilson cloud chamber. This is a device that allows a scientist to look at the tracks made by subatomic particles. The chamber is filled with air or some other gas that has a high concentration of water or alcohol vapor. When charged particles move through the gas, they knock electrons off the molecules that lie in their paths. This changes the molecules to positive ions. Ions are electrically charged atoms or groups of atoms. Vapor collects around the ions. This allows the scientist to see the paths of the subatomic particles. Although the tracks disappear quickly, the scientist can take photographs of them to study.

The cloud chamber was invented in 1911 by British physicist Charles T. R. Wilson. Meitner built the first one in Berlin about ten years later. She used it to look for subatomic particles. She took the first known photographs of traces from a positron.[7]

The time between the end of World War I and 1933 was one of the happiest and most productive in Meitner's life. About her work she wrote,

> There were 25 scientific workers in our [Meitner's and Otto Hahn's] two sections by 1932. . . . A good spirit and a happy mood predominated in this working community . . . which not only had a very favorable impact on the work, but was also expressed time and again, at Christmas and birthday festivities. . . . There existed a strong feeling of belonging together, the basis of which was mutual trust.[8]

Unfortunately, the next year would bring changes in Germany that would end this pleasant time in Meitner's life forever.

# The Rise of the Nazis

ON JANUARY 30, 1933, LISE MEITNER listened on the radio to the swearing-in ceremonies of Adolf Hitler as Germany's new chancellor. His election was the final result of several years of trouble in Germany. After the war, Germany had been governed by the Weimar Republic, a liberal government that sought to increase people's freedoms and rights. The leader of this government, Chancellor Gustav Stresemann, died on October 3, 1929. Just a few weeks later the American stock market crashed. The world was plunged into an economic depression.

Partly as a result of this depression, the National Socialist party, or Nazis, grew more powerful. In the election of 1930 they won many seats in the German governing body called the Reichstag. Nazis believed that what they called the Aryan race was a superior group of people. They thought other races were inferior to them. They blamed these other races, especially Jews, for all of Germany's problems. Even before Hitler came to power, there was much anti-Semitism in Germany from groups like the ones that protested at Einstein's lectures. Anti-Semitism is prejudice against Jewish people.

During this time operations became more difficult at the KWI. Otto Hahn left in February 1933 for the United States, where he had agreed to lecture at Cornell University in New York for a semester. While he was gone, Lise Meitner was in charge of the institute.

As soon as Hitler took office, he began a campaign against all "non-Aryans." Anyone who had at least one Jewish grandparent was considered Jewish. All four of Meitner's grandparents had been Jewish. Even though she had converted to Christianity shortly after moving to Berlin, she was still Jewish according to Nazi law.

Meitner, however, was not too concerned. During the years following World War I, Germany had gone through many social and political upheavals. She may have felt this was another one that would pass without much effect. She also was still an Austrian citizen, which gave her some protection. She continued with her research at the KWI and with her teaching at the University of Berlin.

As the spring wore on, though, the Nazi leadership became more and more difficult to ignore. The new racial laws called for the dismissal of many people Meitner knew in the academic world, including Albert Einstein. Einstein was in the United States when Hitler came to power. On March 10, just before he was about to sail for Europe, he announced he would not be returning to Germany. On March 28, from Belgium, he resigned his position at the

*When Adolf Hitler and the Nazis rose to power in the early 1930s, they made it very difficult for scientists of Jewish ancestry like Lise Meitner to continue working in Germany.*

Prussian Academy of Sciences.[1] He would eventually go to Princeton, New Jersey. Many other scientists began to search for work in other countries, particularly England and Holland. Jobs were hard to find because most countries were in the middle of a terrible economic depression.

In 1933 there were about 600,000 Jews in Germany, which was about 1 percent of the population. In the academic community, though, 20 percent of all scientists and 25 percent of all physicists were Jewish. During April and May, many of these people were dismissed because of the new Nazi policies. There were some exceptions. Those who had been appointed to their jobs before World War I, had served in the war, or had lost a son or father in the war were allowed to keep their jobs.[2]

James Franck, a close friend of Meitner and Hahn, was of Jewish descent. He was allowed to keep his professorship because of his war service. He decided to resign, though, and spoke out against the dismissal of his Jewish colleagues.[3]

Eventually he moved to the United States, where he became a professor at the University of Chicago. Most others were silent, waiting to see what would happen. Some at the KWI began wearing brown shirts to work, the symbol of their membership in the Nazi party.

When Otto Hahn returned from the United States in the summer, he was the new interim director of the KWI. The former director, Fritz Haber, had been forced to resign because he was Jewish. Hahn carried out the work of dismissing many of the workers in the institute and prepared the way for a new Nazi-appointed director, Gerhart Jander, who had done very little research and would not have been considered for the position before the Nazis came to power.[4]

Meitner spent the summer holidays in Vienna, trying to get away from the trouble in Berlin. While she was there she received a questionnaire from the Ministry of Education that, among other things, asked for the race of her four grandparents. At the end of the

*Albert Einstein refused to remain in Germany after Hitler was sworn in as the nation's new chancellor. Einstein eventually settled in Princeton, New Jersey.*

summer, the ministry sent her a letter. It said that, based on the information in her questionnaire, she could no longer teach at the university. Shocked, she asked Otto Hahn and Max Planck to see if they could get the ministry officials to change their minds. Both men wrote letters, but the decision stood. Meitner could no longer give her university lectures.

Meitner's work now was limited to her KWI research. She and Hahn began working with another chemist, Fritz Strassmann. Strassmann was a chemist who had come to the KWI in 1929 for a year's appointment. At the end of the year, he decided he liked it enough to stay a bit longer, even though there was no money to pay him a salary. By 1933 he could not get a job anywhere else because he refused to join any organizations that were associated with the Nazis. Meitner asked Hahn to pay him fifty marks a month, barely enough for food, out of a special fund that could be used by the director.[5]

The research this team was doing had to do with the work of an Italian physicist named

Enrico Fermi. Fermi had recently published some interesting results of experiments he had done with uranium. At this time, uranium was the heaviest known element. Fermi suspected that by bombarding uranium with neutrons, he might form a new, heavier substance. This experiment resulted in the forming of material that he was unable to identify. He believed that this material might be made up of new elements. These elements were called transuranic elements.

Although it had been twelve years since Meitner and Hahn had published an article together, they decided to work together again on this project. Their experiments involved bombarding uranium with neutrons, then dissolving the products in acidic solution and testing them chemically.[6] These experiments required both Meitner's knowledge of physics and Hahn's knowledge of chemistry.

Their work was made more difficult because Meitner was now banned from attending any program at the university that might allow her to keep current in her field. She had to get information secondhand from Hahn or from colleagues living outside of Germany.[7]

The search for transuranic elements was going on in other parts of the world as well. The biggest rivals of the Hahn-Meitner team were Irène Curie (daughter of Marie Curie) and her husband, Frédéric Joliot, who worked in Paris. Both teams of scientists were coming up with different results from similar experiments. But Meitner and Hahn were sure they were right and that the French scientists were wrong.

There was more at stake than simply finding the right answer to a scientific problem. Germany was growing more and more repressive to Jews. Many people, both scientists and non-scientists, spoke out against what they called "Jewish science," which they asserted was false. Meitner and Hahn hoped to use their work to show Germans and the rest of the world what could be accomplished in science, regardless of race or religion. Unfortunately, they would not have a chance to continue in this pursuit.

# Escape from Germany

LISE MEITNER BECAME A GERMAN citizen on March 12, 1938. She had not wanted to become one, but on that day the German army crossed the border into Austria and declared it part of Germany. A crowd of hundreds of thousands greeted Hitler enthusiastically in Vienna that night. The democratic Vienna where Meitner had been born disappeared. All Austrians were immediately considered to be Germans. Jews were taken from their homes, beaten, and killed.[1] They lost most of their rights under the Nazi government. Meitner's Austrian citizenship, which had given her some protection in keeping her position at the KWI, was suddenly gone.

Now Meitner was faced with a very difficult decision. It was unlikely that she could keep working at the KWI. If she were unemployed and tried to leave for another country, she could be arrested and imprisoned. Her friends and colleagues abroad started looking for work for her. Her friend James Franck began the process that would allow her to come to the United States. Meitner decided, though, that she did not want to go anywhere where German was not spoken or understood.[2]

Finally, in early May, she decided to accept an invitation from Niels Bohr to come work at his institute in Copenhagen. She had visited Copenhagen several times and liked the city and the institute. The Bohrs were close friends of hers. Her favorite nephew, Otto Robert Frisch, also a physicist, was working there. When she tried to get a travel visa, though, she found out she could not because her Austrian passport was no longer valid.

Meanwhile, Bohr had contacted two other physicists in Holland: Adriaan Fokker and Dirk Coster. Both worked at Dutch universities. They began a campaign to raise money to pay Meitner's salary to teach in Groningen, where Coster was. Because of the worldwide depression, money was scarce everywhere. Although they were only able to raise a small amount of money, plans began for Meitner's secret escape to Holland.

Another escape plan was also being made. In Stockholm, Sweden, physicist Manne Siegbahn was building the new Research Institute for Physics. Siegbahn had worked with Meitner back in the early 1920s. At Niels Bohr's urging, he agreed to offer her a position. He could not let her know through the mail, though, because there was danger that government censors would read the message. In late June, he sent a messenger, Dr. Rasmussen, to Berlin to let Meitner know.

At the same time, Dirk Coster had decided that Meitner must get out of Germany right away, even if she did not have a job lined up. He wired Peter Debye, the new head of the Kaiser Wilhelm Institute for Physics, that he was coming to interview a new assistant, meaning Meitner. Debye told Meitner about the Dutch offer just after she had heard about the Swedish one. She decided to take the offer to go to Stockholm. Niels Bohr had played a critical role in getting her this position, and she felt loyal to him. Also, nuclear physics in Sweden was just getting started, so she felt she could do more useful work there.[3]

On July 4 Otto Hahn learned that the Nazis were getting stricter about enforcing their rules not to let any German scientists leave the country. He knew he had to get Meitner out right away. The visa for her to go to Sweden had not come through yet, so they contacted Coster to see if he still wanted an "assistant." He arranged for the Dutch border guards to allow

Meitner to come into the country, then left for Berlin on July 11.

After spending the night at the Debye home, Dirk Coster was ready to help Meitner escape. Meanwhile, she still did not know that she was going to Holland instead of Sweden. On the morning of July 12, Hahn called her into his office, told her of the new plans, and said she must leave the next day. Although Meitner was stunned, the two of them agreed to work a normal day. Then she would go back to her hotel room, pack as if she were going on a summer vacation, and leave on the train with Coster. The only people who knew of her plans to escape were Coster, Debye, Hahn, Max von Laue, and another colleague, Paul Rosbaud. Meitner would have no chance to say goodbye to any of her other friends from her thirty years of living in Berlin.

That evening Meitner stayed at the institute until eight o'clock, proofreading a paper to be published by one of her students. Then she went back to her room where she had a little over an hour to pack two small suitcases. She packed only clothes, since she was leaving as if she were taking a vacation. She also had a diamond ring that had belonged to Otto Hahn's mother. He had given it to her at the last minute in case she needed it in an emergency.[4]

On the seven-hour trip to the Dutch border, Meitner experienced the worst tension she had ever known.[5] Although Coster had arranged with the border guards ahead of time to let her cross into Holland, there were Nazis everywhere. She knew that many people who had tried to escape from Germany had been arrested and sent back. Finally the crucial moment arrived. The Dutch guards and the Nazi officials looked over her papers. Then they passed by. She was safe.

She had been in even more danger than she realized. Another scientist at the KWI, Kurt Hess, was also an enthusiastic Nazi who had been trying to get rid of Meitner for quite a while. He had found out about her escape plans and notified the authorities. Fortunately, by the

*Lise Meitner shakes hands with Otto Hahn in 1955. While still in the midst of her uranium experiments with Hahn, Meitner fled Nazi Germany in July 1938. Hahn played a pivotal role in her escape.*

time the allegations were investigated, Otto Hahn could safely report that she was out of the country.[6]

The next day, Dirk Coster sent Otto Hahn a telegram using a prearranged code. He said that his baby had arrived safely. Hahn wired back, saying, "I want to congratulate you. What will be the name of your darling daughter?"[7] Both Meitner and Coster needed a full week of rest to recover from the strain of the escape.

Groningen was a pleasant university town, and a welcome relief from five years of living in Nazi Germany. Meitner spent several weeks there. Finally she decided that she would have more opportunities to continue her research in Sweden. She went by way of Denmark, where she spent several weeks with Niels Bohr and his family. Meitner's decision to leave Holland was a wise one. By 1940 Holland was also taken over by the Nazis, just as Austria had been.

In late August Lise Meitner left Denmark for Sweden. Right before she left, she sent a letter to Otto Hahn, telling him she was officially retiring from the KWI. She hoped that this would allow her to get her pension from her thirty years of work there. With only the two small suitcases she had been able to bring from Germany, she headed for Sweden and a new life. After all her years in Berlin, starting over would not be easy.

# 9

# Splitting the Atom

LISE MEITNER'S ADJUSTMENT TO SWEDEN was difficult. Although Manne Siegbahn welcomed her to his new physics institute, he did not offer much help. The institute was still being built, and it was slow work. Most of her colleagues did not like talking in German, and Meitner was still struggling to learn Swedish. Her salary was low, about the same amount as a young assistant just starting out.[1] Otto Hahn tried to get her pension transferred to Sweden, but he was never able to do so. Worst of all, she had little equipment and no assistants, so it was very difficult for her to continue her work. She became depressed, as she expressed in this letter to Hahn, dated September 25, 1938:

> *Perhaps you cannot fully appreciate how unhappy it makes me to realize that you always think that I am unfair and embittered, and that you also say so to other people. If you think it over, it cannot be difficult to understand what it means to me that I have none of my scientific equipment. For me that is much harder than everything else. But I am not really embittered—it is just that I see no real purpose in my life at the moment and I am very lonely.*[2]

Hahn and Meitner continued their frequent correspondence. In November they had the opportunity to see each other. Niels Bohr invited Hahn to Copenhagen, and Meitner took a train to meet him. Margrethe Bohr, Niels's wife, gave a reception for Hahn on November 10. The next day Meitner, Hahn, Bohr, and Meitner's nephew, Otto Robert Frisch, spent hours discussing their work on the transuranic elements. These elements continued to puzzle Hahn and Fritz Strassmann. Neither Bohr nor Meitner could figure them out, either. Meitner advised Hahn to go back and try the experiments again.

Because of the dangerous situation in Germany, Meitner and Hahn kept this meeting a secret. They never referred to it in their letters to each other, and Hahn did not even tell Strassmann that he had met with Meitner. Strassmann knew that Meitner had urged Hahn to re-check the results, though. He thought she had written to Hahn about it. He still considered her to be the leader of their team.[3] In many ways she still was, since the experiments were being done in her lab using the equipment she had built. She was following all the experiments closely and offering input through her frequent correspondence.[4]

During Hahn's trip to Sweden, more terrible events were happening in Germany. On the night of November 9, Nazis rounded up thousands of Jews in what became known as *Kristallnacht*, the Night of Broken Glass. Jewish businesses were destroyed and people were arrested and taken to concentration camps. New laws were put into place forbidding Jews from selling anything and barring Jewish children from school. In Vienna, Meitner's brother-in-law, Justinian (Jutz) Frisch, was arrested and sent to a concentration camp in Dachau, Germany. Meitner began to make arrangements for her sister, Auguste—Otto Frisch's mother—to join her in Sweden.

Fortunately Jutz Frisch was released in January, and he and his wife came to live in Sweden shortly after that. But the worry before that happened made Christmas a depressing holiday for Meitner. She decided to spend it with her friend Eva von Bahr-Bergius, who lived on the Swedish coast. She also invited Otto Frisch to come up from Copenhagen.

Just before Meitner left, she received a letter from Hahn. He wanted to ask her questions about an experiment he had recently performed with Fritz Strassmann. Still trying to figure out the transuranic elements, they had been working with uranium again. By this point they were anticipating some form of radium to be

*Lise Meitner (right) and Eva von Bahr-Bergius (left).*

among the transuranic elements they produced. But instead they were finding barium, a much lighter element. Part of the uranium's mass had seemed to just disappear. Hahn and Strassmann were completely puzzled. Hahn asked Meitner if she could come up with any ideas.

Meanwhile, Hahn wrote up the findings of

his experiment in an article. He included one paragraph that speculated that the uranium might actually be forming barium and other lighter elements. He could not explain why this was happening. Hahn forwarded a copy of this article to Meitner, but she did not receive it until after Christmas.

On December 21 Frisch arrived from Copenhagen to find his aunt puzzling over another letter Otto Hahn had written on the same subject. Although Frisch was interested in discussing his parents' situation and his own physics work, Meitner was too engrossed in Hahn's experiments. They went outside. Frisch was on skis and Meitner walked alongside him.

As they walked and discussed the problem, they began to see that the nucleus of the atom might actually be able to break apart. They considered Niels Bohr's model of the nucleus, which was like a liquid drop. They realized that one drop could divide itself into two smaller drops. Many scientists had considered Bohr's liquid-drop model before, but none had thought of it splitting. This was a huge leap forward in thinking.

Using this model helped make sense of the heavy uranium turning into lighter elements like barium. The mass of uranium that appeared to disappear was actually being released as energy. Stopping under a tree, Meitner pulled out a piece of paper and pencil and began scribbling calculations. She used Einstein's famous formula relating mass and energy, $E=mc^2$ (energy equals mass times the speed of light squared), to determine the amount of energy being released. Her calculations were astonishing: The amount of energy released in this reaction would be 200 million electron volts per uranium atom.[5]

Although both Hahn and Meitner were slowly moving toward the same conclusions, they were both reluctant to do so. The new idea that the uranium atoms were dividing into lighter elements instead of combining to form the heavier transuranic elements meant that their work of the past three years had all been wrong. On New Year's Day 1939, Meitner wrote to

# Fission

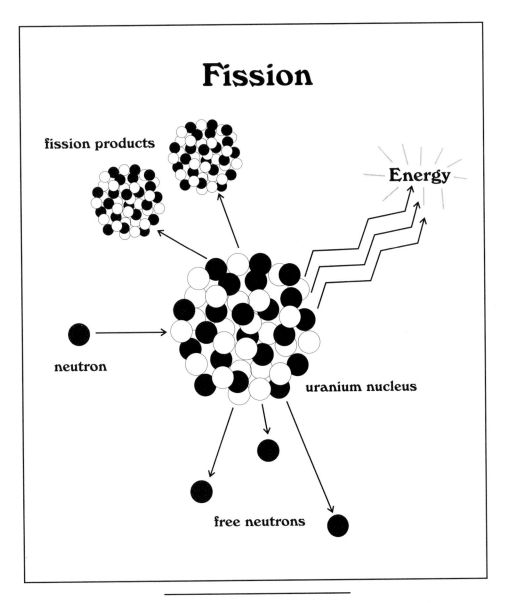

When a neutron splits the nucleus of a uranium atom, the atom's protons and neutrons are released, along with a tremendous amount of energy. Released neutrons will go on and split the nuclei of other atoms in a chain reaction.

Hahn, suggesting that they would have to announce that their work on transuranics had been wrong. She was very worried that this would damage her reputation at her new job.[6] Frisch and Meitner began working on an article to announce their new ideas.

With the new year, both Frisch and Meitner returned to their homes and jobs. Frisch was able to tell Niels Bohr briefly about their discovery. Bohr immediately agreed with everything they had found and was astonished that no one had thought of it sooner.[7] A few days later Frisch and Meitner spoke on the telephone and agreed to begin work on a short article for the British journal *Nature*. They believed this would be the quickest way of communicating their findings with the world's scientific community.[8]

By the beginning of January, the article was ready to be mailed. Frisch was still doing some experiments to confirm their findings and did not send it off right away. Meanwhile, Niels Bohr had left for a trip to America, sailing with his colleague Léon Rosenfeld. Bohr was extremely excited about the discovery Frisch had told him about and spent much of the trip discussing it with Rosenfeld, struggling to understand it completely. By the time they reached the United States, Rosenfeld had a clear understanding of the new findings.

Bohr and Rosenfeld arrived on January 16, which was the same day Frisch mailed the article to *Nature*. Unfortunately, *Nature* did not have room to publish it until the February 11 issue. In the meantime, Rosenfeld, unaware that the news was still somewhat secret, began spreading the word to American physicists. Scientists around the country raced to do experiments to learn more about the splitting of the atom.

On January 22 Frisch wrote a letter to Bohr saying that he was "currently planning various new experiments on these 'fission' processes."[9] This was the first time the word *fission* had been used to describe how the atom was split. Frisch had taken the term from a biochemist friend, William Arnold, who told him that *fission* was the term used to describe the way living cells divided.[10]

On January 26 the news was officially announced to the physics world. Bohr and Enrico Fermi got up at the Fifth Conference on Theoretical Physics in Washington, D.C., and announced the findings of Hahn, Strassmann, Meitner, and Frisch. The room was immediately thrown into chaos. Some of the physicists rushed out of the room to get back to their labs and start new experiments. Journalists attending the meeting reported the news in their papers and magazines. Many of these articles discussed the contributions of Hahn, Bohr, and others to the discovery of fission. Practically none mentioned the name of Lise Meitner.

# 10

# World War II

AT THE KWI, THE POLITICAL SITUATION was getting worse. More and more Nazi scientists were working there. Some of them attacked Otto Hahn for sharing his work on fission with Lise Meitner. Hahn began to distance himself from Meitner and to take more credit for the discovery of fission. Meitner could sense this from their correspondence. This damaged their friendship in a way that would never be fully repaired.[1]

Despite this, Hahn was involved in the frustrating work of sending Meitner her books, furniture, and other belongings. Every time he thought he could send them, a Nazi official would come up with another reason why he could not. The items had to be listed, checked, and re-checked. Finally they arrived in Stockholm. The furniture was broken to splinters, pages had been ripped from books, and china and glassware were smashed.[2]

Hitler continued to expand his power through Europe. In March 1939 he invaded Czechoslovakia. For the next several months world leaders tried to prevent a war. In the world of physics, there was controversy about how much information on fission should be published. Many scientists were worried what would happen if Hitler found out enough to build a "fission bomb."[3] They began to censor what they published. Others, like Frédéric and Irène Joliot-Curie, continued to publish their results.

Leo Szilard was a Hungarian physicist who had emigrated to America in 1938. After reading about Hahn and Meitner's fission experiments, he began a campaign to stop publishing any information that might help Hitler. In August 1939 he went to see Albert Einstein. Together the two of them wrote a letter to President Franklin Roosevelt, explaining the possible dangers of the new nuclear discoveries. They described how a nuclear bomb could be built and mentioned the large uranium sources under Nazi control. Roosevelt wrote back in October, letting Einstein know that he had begun an atomic research program.

In Germany a secret committee was formed on the military uses of fission and uranium. Otto Hahn was one of the senior members. When they started meeting in April 1939, it was clear that Europe would soon be at war.[4]

One of the keys to making an atomic bomb is creating a nuclear chain reaction. This means that uranium atoms will split, releasing neutrons that could split other atoms, so that the fission can keep going. Most scientists believed that this was impossible. Most uranium that occurs in nature is the isotope U-238. The kind needed for a chain reaction is U-235. The scientists believed they would not be able to get enough U-235 to create the reaction. They thought they might be able to have a slow, controlled reaction, but that a faster, uncontrolled reaction necessary for a bomb would be out of reach.[5]

In July 1939 Lise Meitner traveled to Cambridge, England, to consider a new position at the Cavendish Laboratory there. She would also get a contract to teach at Girton College, part of Cambridge University. At first she decided to accept the position, but then she decided to delay her move a year, until the summer of 1940. It was a move she would later regret.[6] By the fall of 1939, Europe was at war again, and moving was impossible.

On September 1, 1939, Hitler invaded Poland. Both England and France had pledged to support Poland. Within a few days, both declared war on Germany. Hitler did not stop his move into Europe with Poland. Soon he invaded Norway and Denmark. Niels Bohr was forced to flee to Sweden, where he helped organize a movement to rescue thousands of

Danish Jews. At Lise Meitner's lab, Manne Siegbahn was involved in secret research for the government on the military applications of fission.[7]

On December 2, 1942, a year after the United States had entered the war, the first nuclear chain reaction took place. Enrico Fermi,

*Lise Meitner speaks to university students in England in 1959. Meitner had considered moving to England to work at the Cavendish Laboratory before World War II broke out in the fall of 1939.*

now working at the University of Chicago, had created a lab in the university's squash courts deep underground. A "pile" of uranium had been constructed. With this, Fermi and his team were able to sustain a chain reaction for twenty-eight minutes.[8]

Not long after this, in 1943, the Manhattan Project became a large-scale operation. This was the name of the top-secret research project in Los Alamos, New Mexico, to create an atomic bomb. That same year Winston Churchill, the prime minister of Great Britain, agreed to combine Britain's atomic research with the Manhattan Project. Otto Robert Frisch, who had been working in Britain, became part of the Manhattan Project team.

Lise Meitner was also invited to join the team in 1943. Although it would have meant an escape from Sweden, where she was unhappy, and a chance to work on an interesting physics project, she strongly stated, "I will have nothing to do with a bomb!"[9] She was one of only a few scientists who did not work for the military

# World War II in Europe

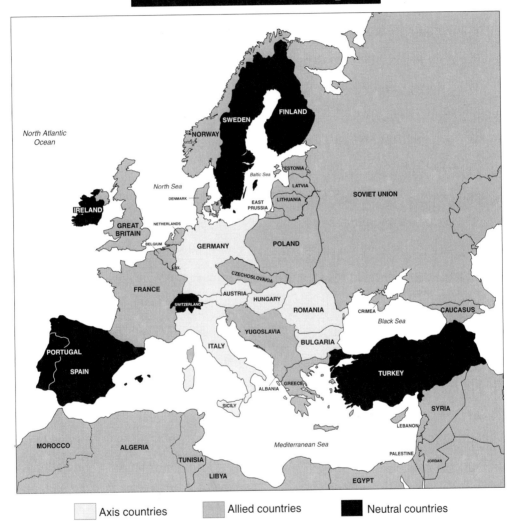

Axis countries     Allied countries     Neutral countries

*World War II began with the German invasion of Poland in 1939. Great Britain and France immediately declared war on Germany. Soon, European nations began siding with either the Allied or Axis powers.*

during World War II. Almost all scientists were motivated by a fear of Hitler and of Germany winning the war. Meitner may have been more influenced by her World War I experiences. She might have been afraid of a bomb being used on Germany, a country she had loved. Whatever the reason, she was quick to refuse the chance to work on the Manhattan Project.[10]

Meitner did worry, however, about the Germans developing a bomb.[11] She also had other worries. Hanno Hahn, Otto Hahn's son and Meitner's godson, was wounded in the war and lost an arm. Max Planck's home was destroyed, and his oldest son, Erwin, was captured and killed by the Nazis for his part in an attempt to assassinate Hitler. Her friends Dirk and Miep Coster were in occupied Holland where people were starving.

In 1944 the Nobel committee voted to award Otto Hahn the Nobel prize for chemistry. Hitler had forbidden any Germans from accepting the Nobel prize. Hahn was notified, but he wrote back that he could not accept the prize.

# Meitner's Legacy

ON MAY 8, 1945, GERMANY SURRENDERED, and World War II ended in Europe. Contact with Germany was cut off, so Lise Meitner did not know what had happened to Otto Hahn and other friends there. In August she took a vacation in the Swedish countryside. On August 6 she received an early morning long-distance telephone call. It was a reporter from a Swedish newspaper. A uranium bomb had been dropped on the city of Hiroshima in Japan.[1]

Within twenty-four hours Meitner became a celebrity. On August 9 a second bomb was dropped, this time on Nagasaki. Newspaper reporters followed Meitner everywhere on her vacation. When she told them she did not know anything about the bomb, they made up stories. One newspaper reported that she had escaped from Germany with the secrets of the atomic bomb and had given them to the Allies. Another claimed the idea of fission had come to her when she was on the train escaping to Sweden. They said that she had telegraphed the idea to her friend Otto Robert Frisch, who told Niels Bohr. Although Meitner struggled to set the record straight, many of these false stories became accepted as fact.[2]

Fortunately she had a chance for some serious radio interviews during which she was able to state her positions. The first was with Eleanor Roosevelt, the First Lady. It took place on August 9, shortly before the bomb was dropped on Nagasaki. Mrs. Roosevelt congratulated Meitner on her work on nuclear fission, and Meitner spoke about the importance of women getting involved in the movement for

*A mushroom cloud forms above Hiroshima, Japan, as a result of the first atomic bomb, dropped on August 6, 1945.*

world peace.[3] Shortly after Nagasaki, Meitner was again interviewed on international radio.

During this time, Meitner found out what had happened to Otto Hahn. He, Max von Laue, and eight other scientists had been taken to England by the British. A country estate called Farm Hall was wired with microphones to secretly record what these men said to each other. They were kept there until the end of 1945. All this was part of the Allied effort to learn how far the fission program in Germany had gone.[4]

In September 1945, shortly after the war in the Pacific ended, Meitner received an invitation to teach for a semester at Catholic University in Washington, D.C. She was grateful for an opportunity to visit the United States without having to move permanently.[5] She also looked forward to a reunion with her two sisters, who lived in the U.S.

Once she arrived in the United States in January 1946, she found herself quite a celebrity. The Women's National Press Club chose her as their Woman of the Year. At the awards ceremony, she ate dinner with President Harry Truman. During the rest of the winter, she lectured at Harvard, Princeton, Wellesley, Massachusetts Institute of Technology (MIT), and several other universities. She became increasingly outspoken on the importance of women in science and of international cooperation among scientists.[6]

After six months in the United States, she returned to Sweden. Shortly before her trip, she had been elected to the Swedish Royal Academy of Sciences, the third woman to become a member in two hundred years. She hoped that this would give her a more secure place in Swedish scientific circles. However, she returned to find very disappointing news.

The Nobel prize, which had not been awarded in 1944, was announced for both 1944 and 1945. Otto Hahn was the winner of the 1944 prize for chemistry for his work in the discovery of nuclear fission. Although Lise Meitner had been nominated with Hahn ten times in the

*Lise Meitner sits alongside President Truman after being honored as Woman of the Year by National Women's Press Club on February 9, 1946.*

past, she was not included this time. Neither was Fritz Strassmann. Many of Meitner's friends and colleagues were on the committee that selected the winners, and the debate was intense. In the end, only Hahn received the prize.

Meitner had the chance to see Otto and Edith Hahn when they came to Sweden for the Nobel prize ceremony. She was shocked when

Hahn spent the whole trip campaigning for aid to Germany. He compared the Allied occupation of Germany after the war with Germany's occupation of Poland and Russia when many, many innocent people were put to death. To Meitner, he seemed to have no sense of remorse over what Germany had done during the war. Instead he focused on how Germany was now suffering. And he never mentioned her name as his co-worker in the work that had earned him the Nobel prize. Their friendship was damaged beyond repair.[7]

The Nobel prize comes with a large amount of money. Otto Hahn gave part of this money to Lise Meitner. She contributed all of it to a committee started by Albert Einstein, the Emergency Committee of Atomic Scientists. This group was concerned about the use of atomic science by governments.

In 1947, Hahn and Fritz Strassmann wrote to Meitner, offering her back her old position at the KWI. Meitner refused the offer. The world was learning the awful details of the Holocaust,

*Otto Hahn and Lise Meitner in September 1955. After World War II, the friendship between Meitner and Hahn became strained. The two would never again be as close as they once were.*

in which 11 million people had died. Meitner felt that the Germans, including Hahn, had not truly come to terms with what they had done. She felt it would be difficult for her to live in Germany again for that reason.[8] She did return in 1949 to receive, with Hahn, the Max Planck Medal, the highest scientific award in Germany.

Although she decided not to move to Germany, Meitner left Manne Siegbahn's institute in 1947. She had never felt welcome there, and she was relieved to be invited to join Sweden's Royal Institute of Technology. She finally had a laboratory of her own, with equipment and assistants. She was able to do interesting work there, including work on Sweden's first experimental nuclear reactor.

Meitner continued to work until 1953, when she retired at age seventy-five. Although she had lost her pension from Germany during the war, she was given retirement benefits from the Swedish government. After her retirement, she continued to attend lectures and seminars and supervise graduate students.

In the late 1950s, Meitner's health began to fail. After she fell and broke her hip, she realized it was too difficult for her to live alone. She moved to Cambridge, England, to be near Otto Robert Frisch and his family. She recovered enough that she was able to travel to Vienna in 1963 to deliver a lecture about her fifty years in physics. Her final long-distance travel was a trip to the United States in 1964, where she had a reunion with her remaining siblings and their families.

In 1966 Meitner became the first woman to receive the Enrico Fermi Award for her contributions to nuclear science. It was awarded jointly to her, Otto Hahn, and Fritz Strassman. With the $15,000 she received from it, she was able to establish a library at Cambridge University. The following year she broke her hip again. This time she was too frail to recover. She died on October 27, 1968, just before her ninetieth birthday. Otto Hahn and his wife, Edith, had both died during the summer of the same year.

*Lise Meitner's headstone.*

Lise Meitner was buried in England, in a cemetery where her favorite brother, Walter, was buried. Otto Robert Frisch chose the inscription on her headstone. It read simply: "Lise Meitner: a physicist who never lost her humanity."

Many years after Meitner's death, a team of German scientists created the heaviest element then known to the world, element 109. In 1992 this element was named meitnerium in honor of Lise Meitner. Peter Armbruster, the leader of the team that discovered meitnerium, said, "Lise Meitner should be honored for her fundamental work on the physical understanding of fission. She should be honored as the most significant woman scientist of this century."[9]

# Activities

### Atom Model

Lise Meitner's work led to a better understanding of the structure of atoms. You can begin to understand the atom's structure by making a model of the lithium atom.

*Materials:*

- Scissors
- 6 people
- String
- A ruler
- Stiff wire
- Modeling clay of three different colors

*Procedure:*

1. Cut two lengths of wire, one twelve inches long and the other eighteen inches long.

2. Twist the ends of each wire together to form two circles.

3.  Arrange the wires so that the smaller circle is inside the larger one.

4.  Press the twisted ends of the wire into a lump of clay so that the circles are standing up.

5.  Cut a six-inch length of string and tie it to the top of the smaller circle. The free end should hang down to the center of the circle.

6.  Choose one color of clay to represent the atom's electrons, one for its protons, and one for its neutrons. Make small balls about the size of the tip of your little finger with the clay. There should be three electrons, three protons, and four neutrons.

7.  Take two electrons. Press one onto each side of the smaller circle. Press the third one onto the outer circle.

8.  Press the protons and neutrons around the free end of the string. You now have a model of a lithium atom.

## Electron Observation

This activity allows you to observe what happens when electrons move around. It works best on a dry day.

*Materials:*

- Two balloons
- Two pieces of string, each three feet long
- A yardstick
- A sweater (optional)

*Procedure:*

1. Inflate two balloons and tie them to the same end of a yardstick.

2. Have a friend hold the other end of the yardstick so that the balloons hang down.

3. Observe the balloons. Do they touch each other?

4. Rub each balloon on your hair or a sweater for thirty seconds.

5. Let the balloons hang down again. What are they doing now?

When you rub the balloons on your hair or a sweater, electrons move onto them. They become negatively charged because they have extra electrons (remember, electrons have a negative charge). Objects that have the same

*Rubbing a balloon on someone's hair causes electrons to move onto the balloon. Hair will then be attracted to the balloon.*

charge repel each other. So the two negatively charged balloons move away from each other.

## The Spectrum

One of the ways Lise Meitner studied atoms was using a spectroscope. A spectroscope breaks down light into separate colors. A rainbow is a spectrum display caused when the sun's rays are broken into colors by raindrops, which act like prisms. You can use a prism to easily make a spectrum, yourself.

*Materials:*

- A prism
- A flashlight or source of natural light
- A smooth wall or other opaque surface

*Procedure:*

1. Shine a light through a prism onto an opaque surface (such as a wall). Observe the way the prism breaks up the light into separate colors. This row of colors is called a spectrum.

# Chronology

1878—Born in Vienna, Austria, on November 7.

1901—Admitted to the University of Vienna.

1906—Earns a Ph.D. in physics from the University of Vienna.

1907—Moves to Berlin, Germany, to begin working at the University of Berlin. Begins working partnership with Otto Hahn.

1912—Moves to the Kaiser Wilhelm Institute in Dahlem, Germany.

1914—World War I begins in Europe.

1915–1917—Serves as a nurse and X-ray technician.

1918—With Otto Hahn, discovers the element protactinium.

World War I ends.

Put in charge of her own physics department.

1925—Promoted to assistant professor.

1938—Escapes Nazi Germany and immigrates to Sweden. Begins working at Manne

Siegbahn's Research Institute for Physics in Stockholm.

1939—With nephew Otto Robert Frisch, publishes an article describing nuclear fission.

1944—Otto Hahn is awarded Nobel prize for Chemistry for the discovery of nuclear fission.

1945—World War II ends with the detonation of the first atomic bombs.

1947—Joins Sweden's Royal Institute of Technology.

1949—Awarded the Max Planck Medal.

1953—Retires from the Sweden's Royal Institute of Technology.

1966—Wins the Enrico Fermi Award with Otto Hahn and Fritz Strassmann.

1968—Dies in Cambridge, England, on October, 27.

1992—Meitnerium, element 109, is named in her honor.

# Chapter Notes

### Chapter 1. A Chain of Events

1. Ruth Lewin Sime, *Lise Meitner: A Life in Physics* (Berkeley, Calif.: University of California Press, 1996), p. 305.

### Chapter 2. Early Years

1. Sallie A. Watkins, "Lise Meitner (1878–1968)," *Women in Chemistry and Physics*, Ed. Louise S. Grinstein, Rose K. Rose, and Miriam H. Rafailovich (Westport, Conn.: Greenwood Press, 1993), p. 394.

2. Lise Meitner, "Looking Back," *Bulletin of the Atomic Scientists*, Vol. 20, November 1964, p. 2.

3. Ruth Lewin Sime, *Lise Meitner: A Life in Physics* (Berkeley, Calif.: University of California Press, 1996), p. 13.

4. Ibid., p. 13.

### Chapter 3. Studying Radiation

1. Lise Meitner, "Looking Back," *Bulletin of the Atomic Scientists*, Vol. 20, November 1964, p. 3.

### Chapter 4. Moving to Berlin

1. Patricia Rife, Lise Meitner and the Dawn of the Nuclear Age (Boston: Birkhauser, 1999), p. 26.

2. Lise Meitner, "Looking Back," *Bulletin of the Atomic Scientists*, Vol. 20, November 1964, p. 5.

3. Rife, p. 33.

4. Ruth Lewin Sime, *Lise Meitner: A Life in Physics* (Berkeley, Calif.: University of California Press, 1996), p 36.

5. Rife, p. 47.

## Chapter 5. The Great War

1. Ruth Lewin Sime, *Lise Meitner: A Life in Physics* (Berkeley, Calif.: University of California Press, 1996), p. 60.

2. Ibid., p. 70.

3. Patricia Rife, *Lise Meitner and the Dawn of the Nuclear Age*. (Boston, MA: Birkhauser, 1999), p. 74.

## Chapter 6. The Calm Before the Storm

1. Ruth Lewin Sime, *Lise Meitner: A Life in Physics* (Berkeley, Calif.: University of California Press, 1996), pp. 98–99.

2. Patricia Rife, *Lise Meitner and the Dawn of the Nuclear Age* (Boston: Birkhauser, 1999), p. 92.

3. Ibid., p. 87.

4. Ibid., pp. 96–97.

5. Ibid., p. 104.

6. Sime, pp. 125–127.

7. Rife, p. 105.

8. Ibid.

## Chapter 7. The Rise of the Nazis

1. Ruth Lewin Sime, *Lise Meitner: A Life in Physics* (Berkeley, Calif.: University of California Press, 1996), p. 137.

2. Ibid., p. 139.

3. Patricia Rife, *Lise Meitner and the Dawn of the Nuclear Age* (Boston: Birkhauser, 1999), p. 112.

4. Sime, p. 146.

5. Ibid., pp. 156–157.

6. Rife, p. 147.

7. Ibid., p. 134.

## Chapter 8. Escape from Germany

1. Ruth Lewin Sime, *Lise Meitner: A Life in Physics* (Berkeley, Calif.: University of California Press, 1996), p. 184.

2. Patricia Rife, *Lise Meitner and the Dawn of the Nuclear Age* (Boston: Birkhauser, 1999), p. 164.

3. Sime, p. 201.

4. Ibid., p. 204.

5. Rife, p. 173.

6. Sime, p. 205.

7. Rife, p. 173.

## Chapter 9. Splitting the Atom

1. Ruth Lewin Sime, *Lise Meitner: A Life in Physics* (Berkeley, Calif.: University of California Press, 1996), p. 214.

2. Patricia Rife, *Lise Meitner and the Dawn of the Nuclear Age* (Boston: Birkhauser, 1999), p. 179.

3. Sime, p. 229.

4. Ibid., p. 234.

5. Rife, pp. 189–190.

6. Sime, p. 141.

7. Rife, p. 198.

8. Ibid.

9. Ibid., p. 205.

10. Frisch, Otto R., "How It All Began," *Physics Today*, November, 1967, p. 48.

## Chapter 10. World War II

1. Patricia Rife, *Lise Meitner and the Dawn of the Nuclear Age* (Boston: Birkhauser, 1999), pp. 212–213.

2. Ruth Lewin Sime, *Lise Meitner: A Life in Physics* (Berkeley, Calif.: University of California Press, 1996), pp. 268–270.

3. Rife, p. 223.

4. Sime, p. 277.

5. Ibid., p. 276.

6. Ibid., p. 278.

7. Rife, p. 232.

8. Ibid., pp. 234–235.

9. Sime, p. 305.

10. Ibid., pp. 305–306.

11. Ibid., p. 307.

## Chapter 11. Meitner's Legacy

1. Ruth Lewin Sime, *Lise Meitner: A Life in Physics* (Berkeley, Calif.: University of California Press, 1996), p. 313.

2. Ibid., pp. 314–315.

3. Patricia Rife, *Lise Meitner and the Dawn of the Nuclear Age* (Boston: Birkhauser, 1999), pp. 252–253.

4. Leslie R. Groves, *Now It Can Be Told: The Story of the Manhattan Project* (New York: Harper and Brothers, 1962), pp. 247, 337–338.

5. Rife, p. 253.

6. Ibid., p. 255.

7. Sime, p. 341.

8. Rife, pp. 261–262.

9. Sharon Bertsch McGrayne, *Nobel Prize Women in Science* (New York: Birch Lane Press, 1993), p. 63.

# Glossary

**actinium**—A radioactive metal formed by the decay of the uranium isotope U-235.

**alpha particle**—A positively charged particle given off by the nucleus of an atom during nuclear transformation.

**atomic mass**—The sum of the number of protons and neutrons in one atom of a particular element.

**atomic number**—The number of protons in one atom of a particular element.

**atoms**—The particles that make up the basic chemical elements.

**beta particle**—A particle given off by the nucleus of an atom during nuclear transformation. Most beta particles are electrons, but they can sometimes be positrons.

**chain reaction**—A series of events where each action initiates the next.

**electrons**—Subatomic particles with a negative charge that orbit the nucleus of an atom. Electrons have almost no mass and therefore do not contribute to the atomic mass of an element.

**fission**—An energy-producing process in which atoms are split.

**gamma rays**—A form of radiation similar to X-rays.

**hydrogen**—The lightest, simplest element in nature.

**ion**—An atom or group of atoms that are electrically charged. Atoms and molecules become charged if they gain or lose electrons. Gaining electrons will give an atom a negative charge. Losing electrons will give a positive charge.

**isotope**—One of two or more forms of the same element that possess different atomic masses. At the nuclear level, an isotope has the same number of protons as the base element, but a different number of neutrons.

**law**—In science, a generalization of the way nature appears to act.

**mechanics**—A field of physics in which scientists study the effects of forces on different matter, either at rest or in motion.

**meitnerium**—One of the heaviest and most complex synthetic (human-made) elements. This element was named in honor of Lise Meitner.

**neutrons**—Subatomic particles that have neither a positive nor a negative charge. Along with protons, neutrons make up part of the nucleus of an atom.

**nuclear**—Of or relating to the nucleus of an atom or atoms.

**nuclear transformation**—A change that occurs in an atom or atoms.

**nucleus**—The central part of an atom. It contains protons and neutrons.

**particle**—Any of the basic units of matter and energy.

**positron**—A particle equal in mass to an electron but with a positive charge.

**protactinium**—A radioactive metal occurring naturally in all uranium ores.

**protons**—Subatomic particles that have a positive charge. Along with neutrons, they make up the nucleus of an atom.

**radiation**—The particles or energy given off by an atom when it is undergoing nuclear transformation.

**radioactive**—The property of emitting particles or energy.

**radioactive decay**—The transformation of an element due to a change in the number of protons and neutrons in its atoms.

**ray**—A stream of material particles or radiation traveling in the same line.

**scattering**—The process of observing collisions between atomic or subatomic particles.

**spectrometer**—An instrument that measures wavelengths of light.

**tantalum**—A very rare metallic element.

**thermodynamics**—The study of different kinds of energy and of the conversion of energy from one form into another.

**transuranic**—Any of the elements derived from the nuclear transformation of uranium.

**uranium**—A silver-colored radioactive metal that is the heaviest natural element, with an atomic number of 92. There are three different isotopes of uranium. The lightest isotope has 142 neutrons, giving it an atomic mass of 234 (142 neutrons plus 92 protons). This isotope is called U-234. In the other two isotopes, one has 143 neutrons (U-235), and the other has 146 neutrons (U-238).

**X-rays**—A form of electromagnetic radiation.

# Further Reading

Barron, Rachel. *Lise Meitner: Discoverer of Nuclear Fission*. Greensboro, N.C.: Morgan Reynolds, Incorporated, 1999.

Fox, Karen. *The Chain Reaction: Pioneers of Nuclear Science*. Danbury, Conn.: Franklin Watts, Inc., 1998.

Gardner, Robert. *Science Projects About Physics in the Home*. Berkeley Heights, N.J.: Enslow Publishers, Inc., 1999.

Goldenstern, Joyce. *Albert Einstein: Physicist and Genius*. Berkeley Heights, N.J.: Enslow Publishers, Inc., 1995.

Graham, Ian. *Nuclear Power*. Orlando, Fla.: Raintree Steck-Vaughn Publishers, 1999.

Hewitt, Sally. *Forces Around Us*. Danbury, Conn.: Children's Press, 1998.

Poynter, Margaret. *Marie Curie: Discoverer of Radium*. Berkeley Heights, N.J.: Enslow Publishers, Inc., 1994.

Wingate, Philippa. *Essential Physics*. Tulsa, Okla.: E D C Publishing, 1999.

# Internet Addresses

**Lise Meitner Online**
http://www.users.bigpond.com/Sinclair/fission/
    LiseMeitner.html

**The ABC's of Nuclear Science**
http://www.lbl.gov/abc/

**Atomic Alchemy: Nuclear Processes**
http://library.thinkquest.org/17940/

# Index

**A**

actinium, 42–43
alpha ray, 24–25
Armbruster, Peter, 106
atomic bomb, 7, 89, 92, 95–96
atomic energy, 53
atomic mass, 23, 26
atomic number, 23–24
atoms, 7–9, 23, 53, 82, 85

**B**

Bahr-Bergius, Eva von, 33, 79
Berlin, Germany, 35, 48
Bohr, Niels, 47, 68, 70, 81, 90
Boltzmann, Ludwig, 16–18, 30

**C**

Cambridge University, 90, 104
Chadwick, James, 54
chain reaction, 9, 89, 92
concentration camps, 78–79

Copenhagen Institute, 51, 68
Coster, Dirk, 47, 69, 71
Curie, Irène, 66, 88

**D**

deuterium atom, 24

**E**

Einstein, Albert, 46, 48, 53, 59, 89
electrons, 23, 25–26, 51–53
energy, 7, 53

**F**

Farm Hall, 98
Fermi, Enrico, 65, 85, 91–92
Fischer, Emil, 31–32, 36
fission, nuclear, 7, 83, 85–86, 91, 96, 99, 106
Franck, James, 61–62, 68
Frisch, Otto Robert, 68, 77, 79, 81, 92

**G**

gamma rays, 26

Great Britain, 54, 92
gymnasiums, 13

## H

Hahn, Otto, 30–33, 37, 38, 45, 49, 70, 76–77, 94, 99, 104
Hiroshima, Japan, 7, 95
Hitler, Adolf, 57, 67, 88, 90, 94
Holland, 69, 71, 74
Holocaust, 101–103
hydrogen atoms, 23–24

## I

Ignaz Lieber Prize, 49
ions, 55
isotopes, 24, 89–90

## J

Joliot, Frédéric, 66, 88

## K

Kaiser Wilhelm Institute (KWI), 37, 41, 45, 51, 87
Kristallnacht, 78

## L

Laue, Max von, 49, 71
Leibniz Prize, 49

## M

Manhattan Project, 10, 92, 94
Meitner, Lise
    discovery of fission, 76–86
    discovery of radiation, 21–28
during World War I, 38–47
during World War II, 87–94
early years of, 11–20
escape from Germany, 67–75
flourishing career of, 47–56
legacy of, 95–106
rise of Nazism and, 57–66
work in Berlin, 29–37

## N

Nagasaki, Japan, 95, 96
Nazism, 48, 58–59, 61, 67, 70, 78
neutrons, 9, 22–23, 26, 53–55, 65, 89
Nobel prize, 49, 99–101
nuclear reactions, 54, 89–90
nucleus, 22, 51, 53, 81

## P

particles, 26, 55
Planck, Max, 26–28, 29, 46, 49
positrons, 25–26, 55
protactinium, 45
protons, 22, 25–26, 51

## R

radiation, 24–26, 43, 53
radioactive, 22, 24, 42
radioactive decay, 22
Rosenfeld, Léon, 84–85

Rubens, Heinrich, 33, 49
Rutherford, Ernest, 31, 32, 51

## S

scattering, 26
Siegbahn, Manne, 47, 69, 76, 91
spectrometer, 53
Stockholm, Sweden, 69, 71, 74, 76
Strassmann, Fritz, 64, 77
Szilard, Leo, 88–89

## T

tantalum, 42
thermodynamics, 29
transuranic elements, 65–66, 77
tritium atom, 24

## U

University of Berlin, 29, 35, 49, 59
University of Prague, 39
University of Vienna, 14–16, 18
uranium, 42, 65, 79–82, 89, 92

## V

Vienna, Austria, 11, 67, 79

## W

Wilson, Charles T. R., 55
World War I, 38, 47, 59, 61
World War II, 7, 90, 91, 94, 95, 101

## X

X-rays, 39